Learn the Alphabet and Numbers with Gopi

This book belongs to

HarperCollinsChildren'sBooks

First published in India in 2021 by HarperCollins Children's Books

An imprint of HarperCollins *Publishers*
A-75, Sector 57, Noida, Uttar Pradesh 201301, India
www.harpercollins.co.in

2 4 6 8 10 9 7 5 3 1

P-ISBN: 978-93-5422-849-0

This book includes illustrations from *The Gopi Diaries: Coming Home*, the first book in the bestselling The Gopi Diaries series, written by Sudha Murty and illustrated by Sandhya Prabhat. Illustrations other than the ones from The Gopi Diaries series are by Sukriti Sobti.

The Gopi Diaries logo on the front cover (left) designed by Shamika Chaves with text and illustrations by Sandhya Prabhat; the Gopi Early Learning logo on the front cover (right) designed by Sukriti Sobti

Printed and bound at Thomson Press (India) Ltd

Sukriti Sobti is a graphic designer with several years of experience in the book publishing industry. Currently based in Vancouver, Canada, Sobti has previously worked with leading publishing houses such as Dorling Kindersley and has been creating and designing content for children. She has a Masters Degree in English Literature from Jamia Milia Islamia and a Post-graduate Diploma in Graphics and Animation from the same university.

Learn the Alphabet and Numbers with Gopi

Designed and compiled by

Sukriti Sobti

HarperCollinsChildren'sBooks

Use a pencil to trace the letter A.
Then try and write it on your own.

Aa

Aa Aa

A A A A A A

a a a a a a a

Help Gopi reach the water bowl by colouring the boxes with capital letter A and small letter a.

A	a	A	c	E	v	k	d	N	
	p	a	A	a	M	k	l	q	
	L	o	F	A	a	A	a	j	
	y	H	B	g	s	t	A	a	a

Identify the object and fill in the box with capital A or small a. Then read out loud the name of the object.

☐ pple

H ☐ t

Trace the missing letters to complete the sentence. Then read it out loud.

Ants do not have ears.

Use a pencil to trace the letter B.
Then try and write it on your own.

Bb

Bb Bb

B B B B B B B

b b b b b b b

Colour the stars with capital B pink and small b blue.
One has been done for you.

b B b B b

B b B b B

Circle the pictures that begin with the letter B.

Peas

Rabbit

Boat

Ball

Bell

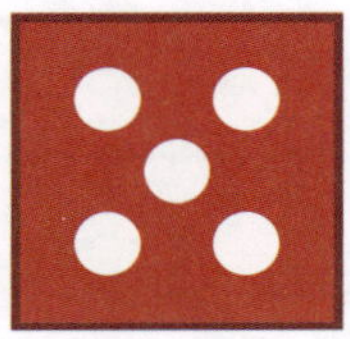
Board Game

Trace the missing letters to complete the sentence.
Then read it out loud.

Bees have five eyes.

Use a pencil to trace the letter c.
Then try and write it on your own.

Cc

Join the circles with capital C and small c to make a pattern.

C o c S c Q

p c R C n C

Colour the objects that begin with the letter C.

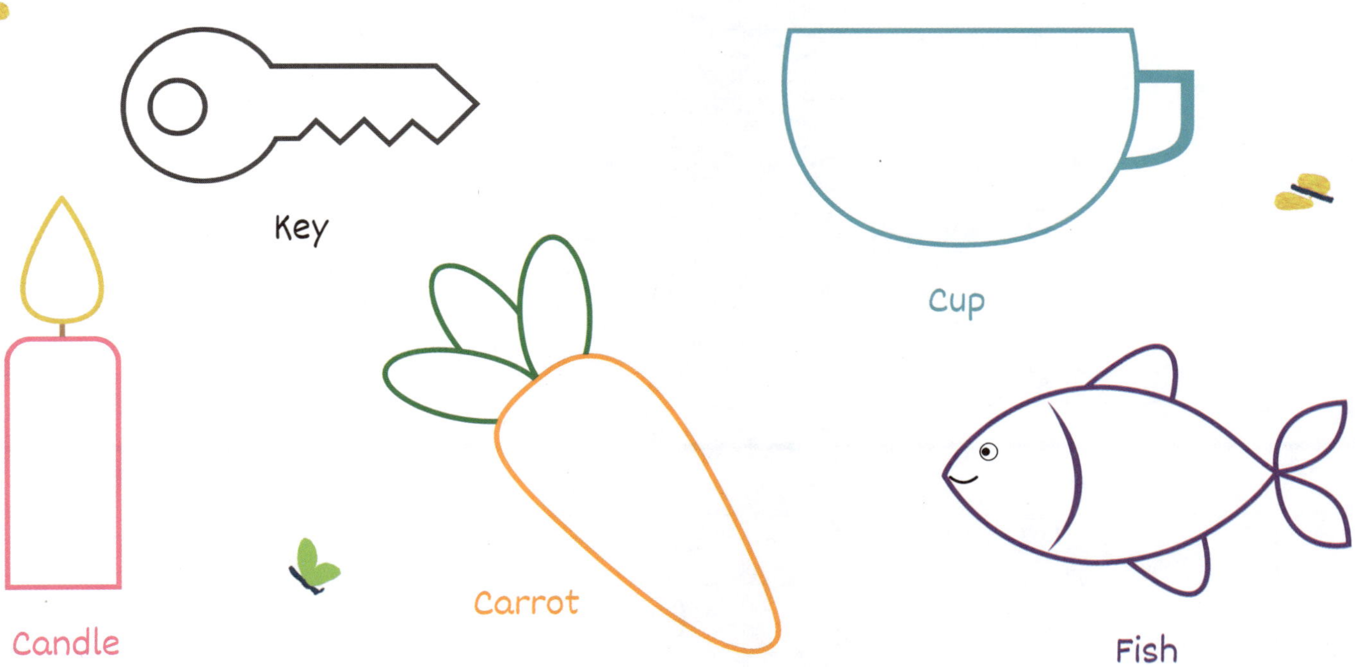

Trace the missing letters to complete the sentence.
Then read it out loud.

Cats walk on their toes.

Dd

Use a pencil to trace the letter D.
Then try and write it on your own.

D d D d

D D D D D D

d d d d d d d

Trace the outline of the shapes with capital D and small d.

Write capital D to complete the word.
Match the word with the correct picture.

____ ress   ____ uck   ____ og   ____ rum

Trace the missing letters to complete the sentence. Then read it out loud.

Dogs love to be around people.

Identify the small letter that matches each capital letter and trace the shape around it.

A	e	a	p
B	b	d	r
C	g	c	j
D	k	b	d

Trace the missing letters to complete the words. Then read them out loud.

was   and   but

bed   can   act

did   dad   find

Trace the first letter for each of the images below.

Ant

Butterfly

Cake

Dolphin

Write the letters in the correct order in the blank puzzle pieces.
Then colour the jigsaw to complete it.

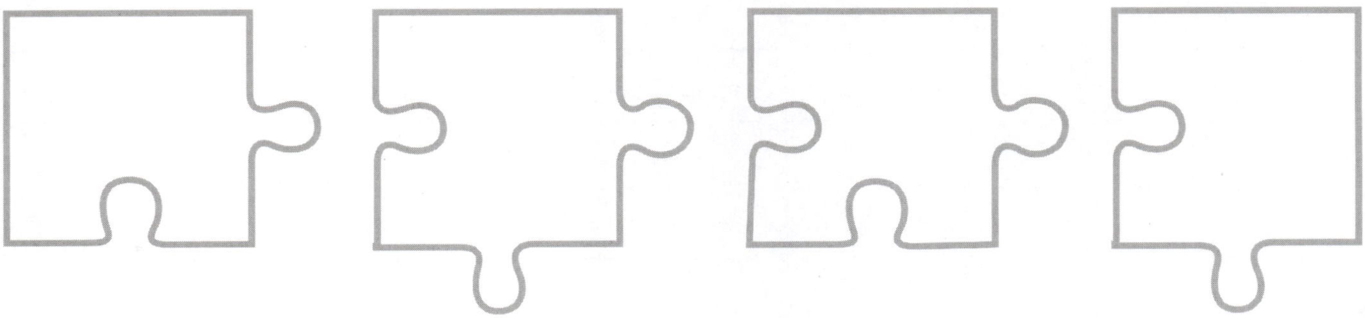

Use a pencil to trace the letter E.
Then try and write it on your own.

Ee

Colour the circles with capital E and small e.

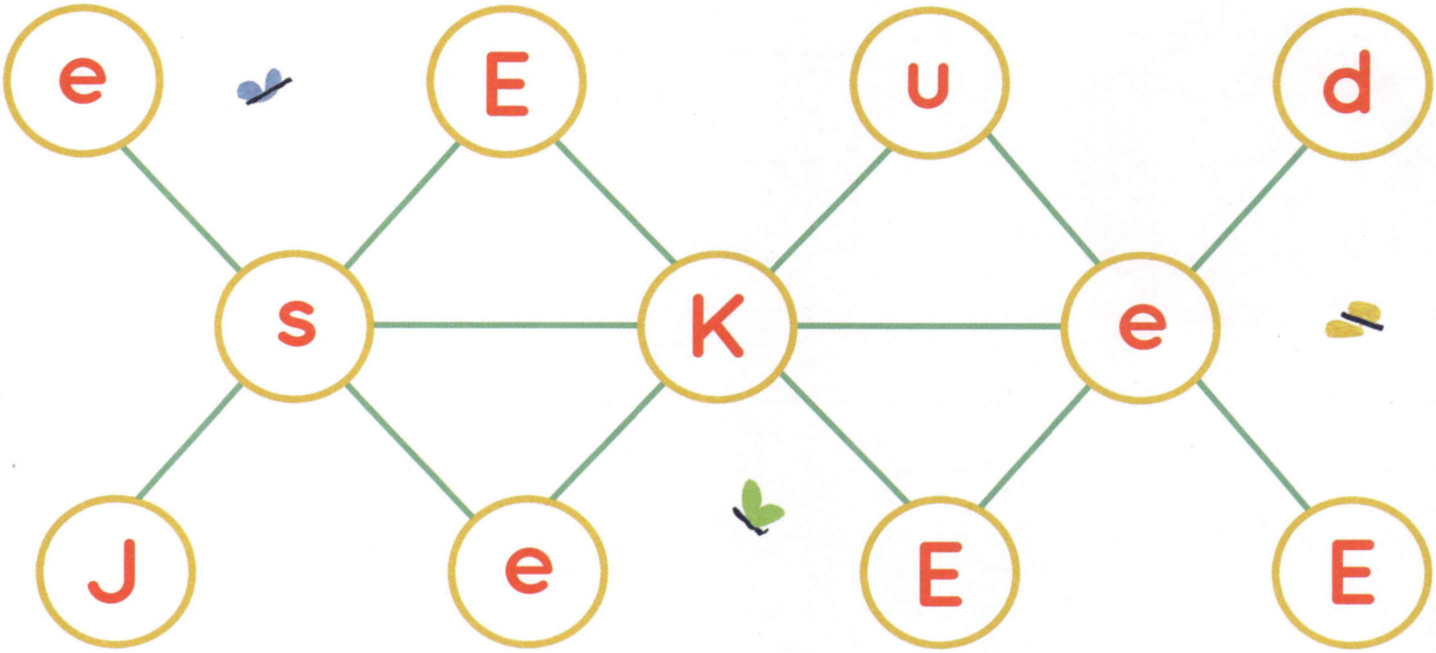

Identify the object and fill in the box
with capital E or small e.

☐ ggplant

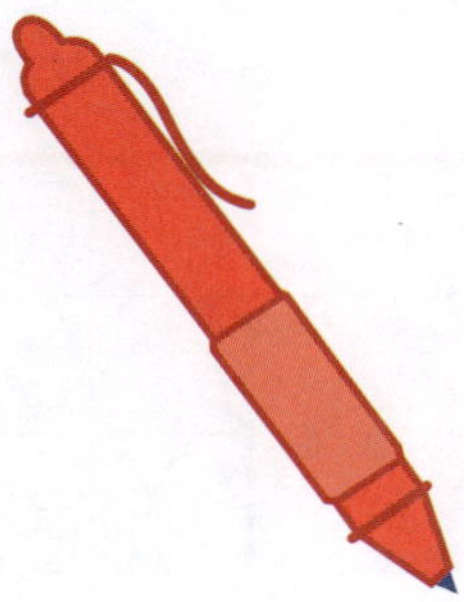

P ☐ n

Trace the missing letters to complete the sentence.
Then read it out loud.

Elephants cannot jump.

Use a pencil to trace the letter F.
Then try and write it on your own.

Ff

F f F f

Colour the leaves with capital F green and small f orange.
One has been done for you.

F f F f f

f F f F F

Circle the pictures that begin with the letter F.

Flower

Food

Vase

Ice Cream

Frog

Triangle

Trace the missing letters to complete the sentence.
Then read it out loud.

Flamingos are pink in colour.

Use a pencil to trace the letter G.
Then try and write it on your own.

G g G g

G G G G G G

g g g g g g g

Colour the objects that begin with the letter G.

Guava

Snake

Watering can

Grapes

Join the circles with capital G and small g to make a pattern.

Y	x	g	G	c	s
G	g	H	m	g	G

Trace the missing letters to complete the sentence. Then read it out loud.

Giraffes eat leaves.

Use a pencil to trace the letter H.
Then try and write it on your own.

Hh

Trace the outline of the balloons with capital H and small h.

Write capital H to complete the word. Match the word with the correct picture.

___ at ___ ammer ___ ouse ___ eart

Trace the missing letters to complete the sentence. Then read it out loud.

Horses can sleep standing up.

Choose the capital letter from the boxes and write it in the space provided.

E F G H

g ___ h ___ e ___ f ___

Write the missing capital letters to help the butterfly reach the flowers.

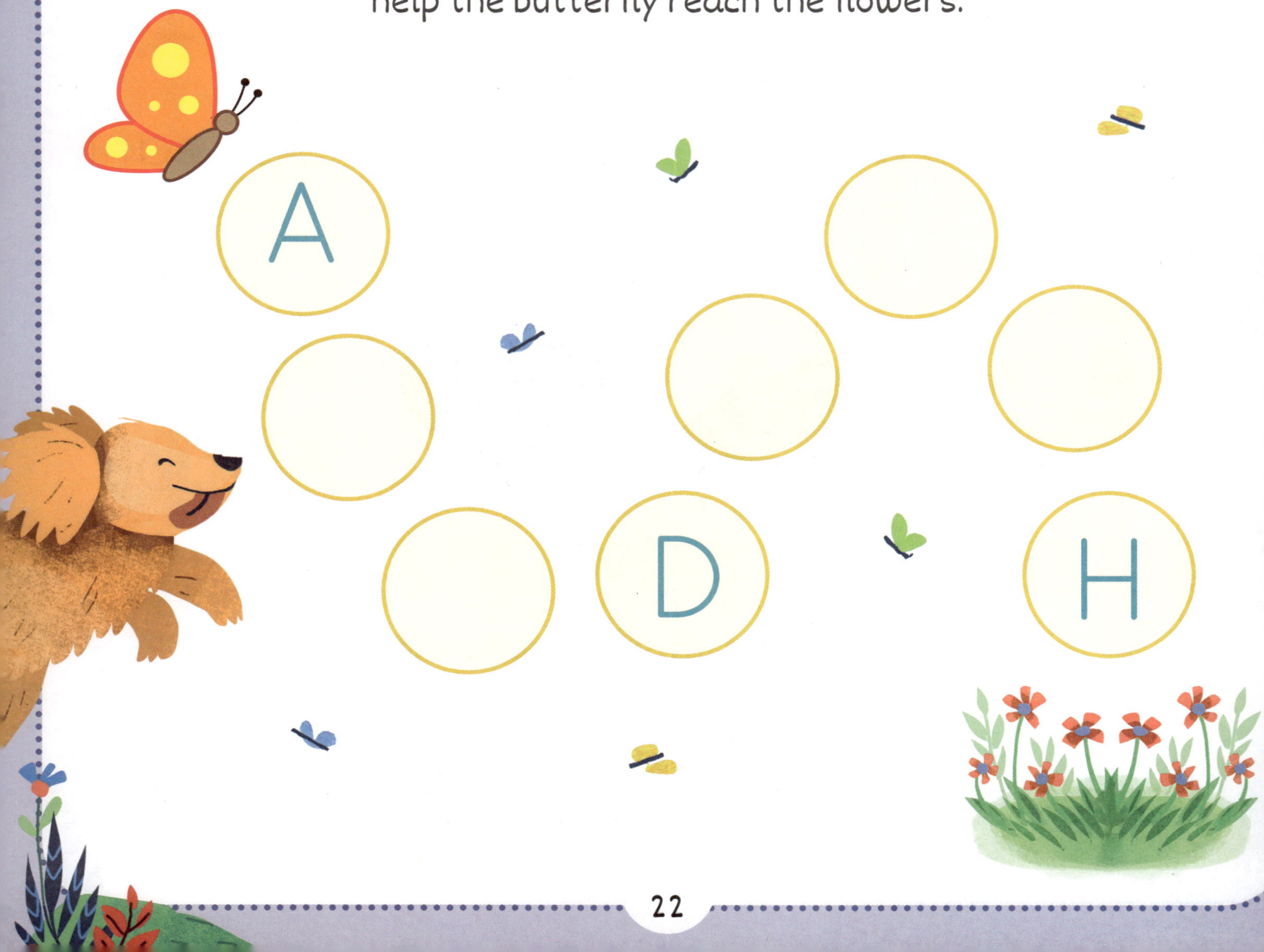

Trace the first letter for each of the images below.

Egg

Fire

Grass

Hanger

Trace the missing letters to complete the words.
Then read them out loud.

eat easy fly

feet go gate

has hide hot

Use a pencil to trace the letter I.
Then try and write it on your own.

Ii

I i I i

I I I I I I I I I

i i i i i i i i i

Identify the object and fill in the box with capital I or small i.

☐ nk

p ☐ n

Colour the boxes with capital I and small i.

M	d	I	i	I	i	I	q	L
g	P	t	J	i	S	k	Z	c
A	h	N	x	I	r	O	b	U
w	E	y	C	i	F	d	G	a
o	K	p	n	I	v	e	S	H
F	b	i	I	i	I	i	B	m

Trace the missing letters to complete the sentence. Then read it out loud.

Igloos are snow houses.

Use a pencil to trace the letter J.
Then try and write it on your own.

Jj

Colour the lemons with capital J yellow and small j orange. One has been done for you.

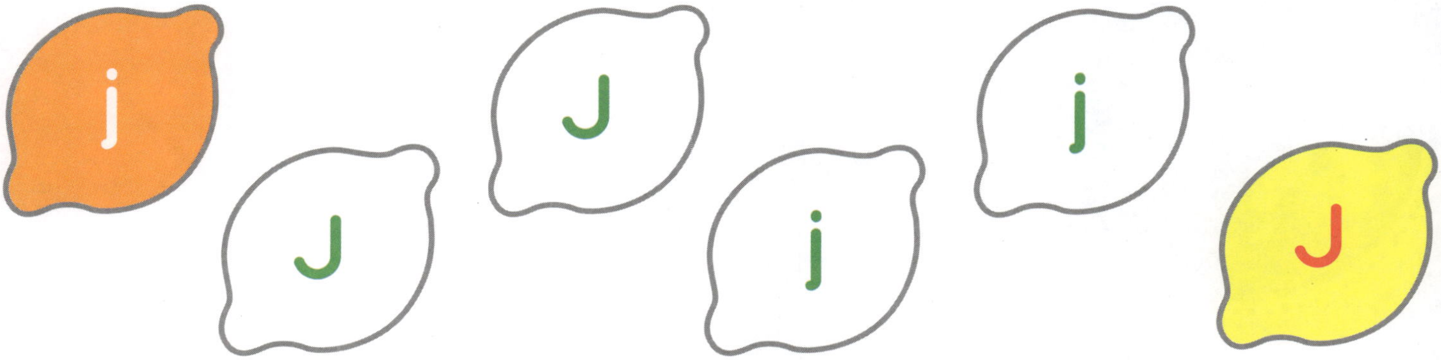

Circle the pictures which begin with the letter J.

Trace the missing letters to complete the sentence. Then read it out loud.

Jellyfish do not have eyes.

Use a pencil to trace the letter K.
Then try and write it on your own.

Kk

K k K k

K K K K K K

k k k k k k k

Colour the pictures that begin with the letter K.

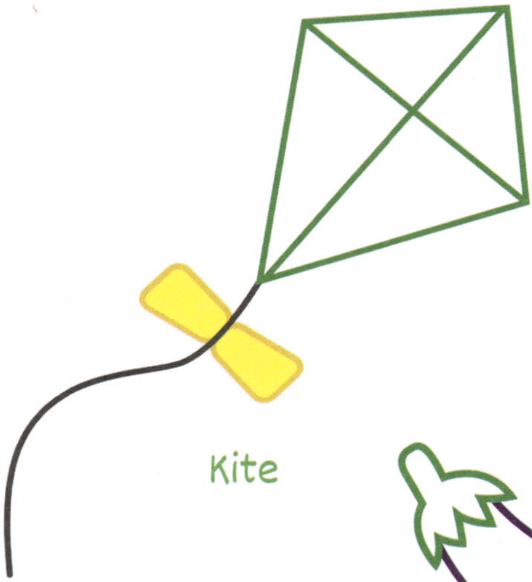

Kite

Quill

Flower

Eggplant

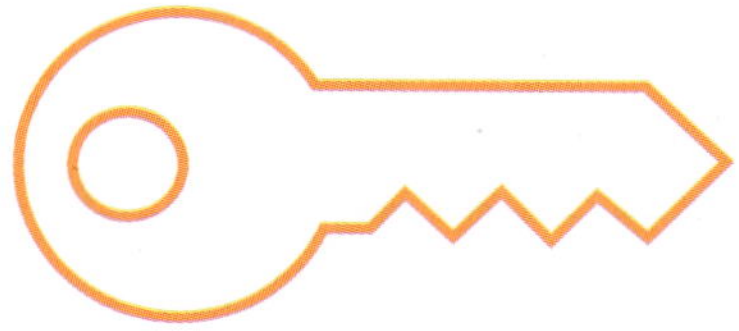

Key

Join the circles with capital K and small k to make a pattern.

K	k	v	A	K	k
s	F	K	k	t	B

Trace the missing letters to complete the sentence. Then read it out loud.

Kiwi birds cannot fly.

Use a pencil to trace the letter L.
Then try and write it on your own.

Ll

Trace the outline of the shape with capital L and small l.

Write capital L to complete the word.
Match the word with the correct picture.

___emon ___eaf ___amp ___adybug

Trace the missing letters to complete the sentence. Then read it out loud.

Lollipop is a sugar candy.

Identify and circle the correct capital letter.

i	T	V	I
j	G	J	A
k	K	D	F
l	Y	S	L

Write the missing capital letters in the blocks.

	A			
		E		
H				L

Trace the first letter for each of the images below.

Ice

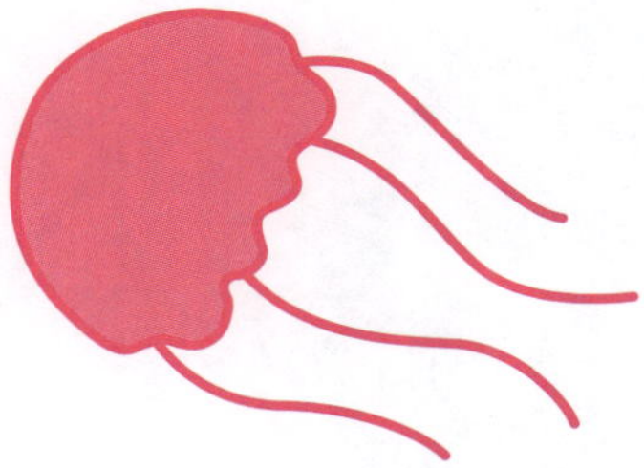

Jellyfish

Kiwifruit

Lock

Trace the missing letters to complete the words.
Then read them out loud.

it is if

just jump kind

kick look lamb

Use a pencil to trace the letter M.
Then try and write it on your own.

Mm

Mm Mm

M M M M M M

m m m m m m m

Help the squirrel reach the nut by tracing a path with capital M and small m.

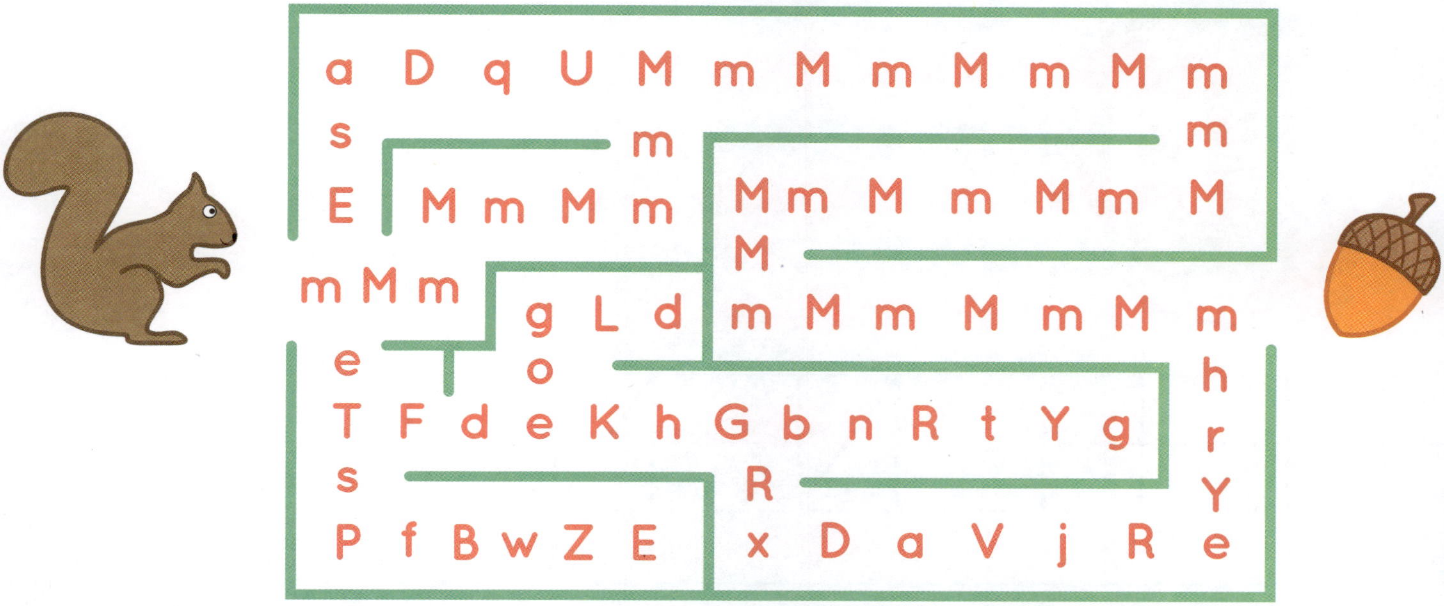

Identify the object and fill in the box with capital M or small m.

☐ ango

Ja ☐

Trace the missing letters to complete the sentence. Then read it out loud.

Mango is a summer fruit.

Use a pencil to trace the letter N.
Then try and write it on your own.

Nn

N n N n

N N N N N N

n n n n n n n

Colour the apples with capital N green and small n red.
One has been done for you.

Circle the pictures which begin with the letter N.

Trace the missing letters to complete the sentence. Then read it out loud.

Nighttime is for dreams.

O o

Use a pencil to trace the letter O.
Then try and write it on your own.

Join the circles with capital O and small o to make a pattern.

M O d O o O

p o O o F g

Colour the objects that begin with the letter O.

Octopus

Orange

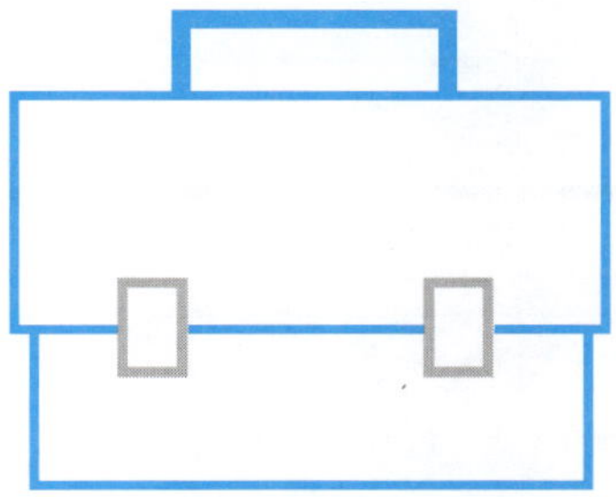

Bag

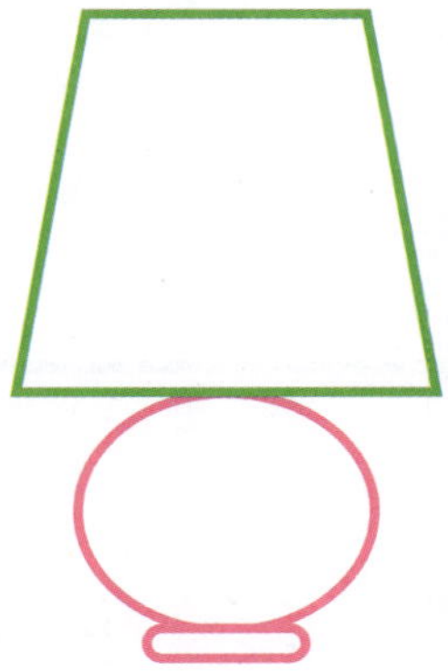

Lamp

Trace the missing letters to complete the sentence. Then read it out loud.

Ostrich is the world's largest bird.

Use a pencil to trace the letter P.
Then try and write it on your own.

Pp

Pp Pp

P P P P P P P

p p p p p p p p p

Trace the outline of the clouds with capital P and small p.

P o p

m P A

Write capital P to complete the word.
Match the word with the correct picture.

___ en   ___ ear   ___ eas   ___ izza

Trace the missing letters to complete the sentence. Then read it out loud.

Pumpkin is a fruit.

Choose the capital letter from the boxes and write it in the space provided.

M N O P

o ___ m ___ p ___ n ___

Write the missing capital letters to complete the picture of the caterpillar.

Trace the first letter for each of the images below.

Moon

Nib

Olive

Pencil

Trace the missing letters to complete the words.
Then read them out loud.

map man net

nose one owl

pie paint many

Use a pencil to trace the letter Q.
Then try and write it on your own.

Qq

Colour the triangles with capital Q and small q.

k G Q q A

q Q R Q s

Identify the object and fill in the box with capital Q.

☐ueen

☐uill

Trace the missing letters to complete the sentence. Then read it out loud.

Quail eggs are small in size.

Use a pencil to trace the letter R.
Then try and write it on your own.

Rr

Rr Rr

R R R R R R R

r r r r r r r r

Colour the flowers with capital R pink and small r purple.
One has been done for you.

Circle the pictures which begin with the letter R.

Hanger

Ring

Ladybug

Rabbit

Duck

Rocket

Trace the missing letters to complete the sentence. Then read it out loud.

Raspberries are red in colour.

Use a pencil to trace the letter s.
Then try and write it on your own.

Ss

Colour the objects that begin with the letter S.

Snake

Cloud

Hat

Sun

Join the circles with capital S and small s to make a pattern.

X	r	s	S	c	z
s	S	G	b	s	S

Trace the missing letters to complete the sentence. Then read it out loud.

Spiders spin webs to catch bugs.

Use a pencil to trace the letter T.
Then try and write it on your own.

Tt

Trace the outline of the shapes with capital T and small t.

Write capital T to complete the word.
Match the word with the correct picture.

___eapot ___urtle ___wo ___omato

Trace the missing letters to complete the sentence. Then read it out loud.

Trees help us breathe.

Use a pencil to trace the letter U.
Then try and write it on your own.

Uu

Identify the object and fill in the box with capital U and small u.

☐ mbrella

B ☐ g

Help the rabbit reach the carrot by colouring the boxes with capital letter U and small letter u.

	h	V	U	u	U	r	G	k	
	B	p	u	d	u	y	u	U	u
	U	u	U	w	U	t	U	a	
U	u	Z	x	S	u	U	u	M	

Trace the missing letters to complete the sentence. Then read it out loud.

Umbrellas protect us from rain.

Choose the capital letter from the boxes and write the corresponding small letter of each of these capital letters.

Q R S T U

_____ _____ _____ _____ _____

Write the missing capital letters to help the honey bee reach the pot of honey.

Identify and circle the correct first letter for each of the images below.

Sun   U   B   S

Tomato   G   T   C

Rabbit   R   G   E

Umbrella   J   N   U

Trace the missing letters to complete the words. Then read them out loud.

quiz   queen   red

rest   sea   stay

toy   tent   use

Use a pencil to trace the letter V.
Then try and write it on your own.

Vv

Colour the mittens with capital V blue and small v orange. One is done for you.

Circle the pictures which begin with the letter V.

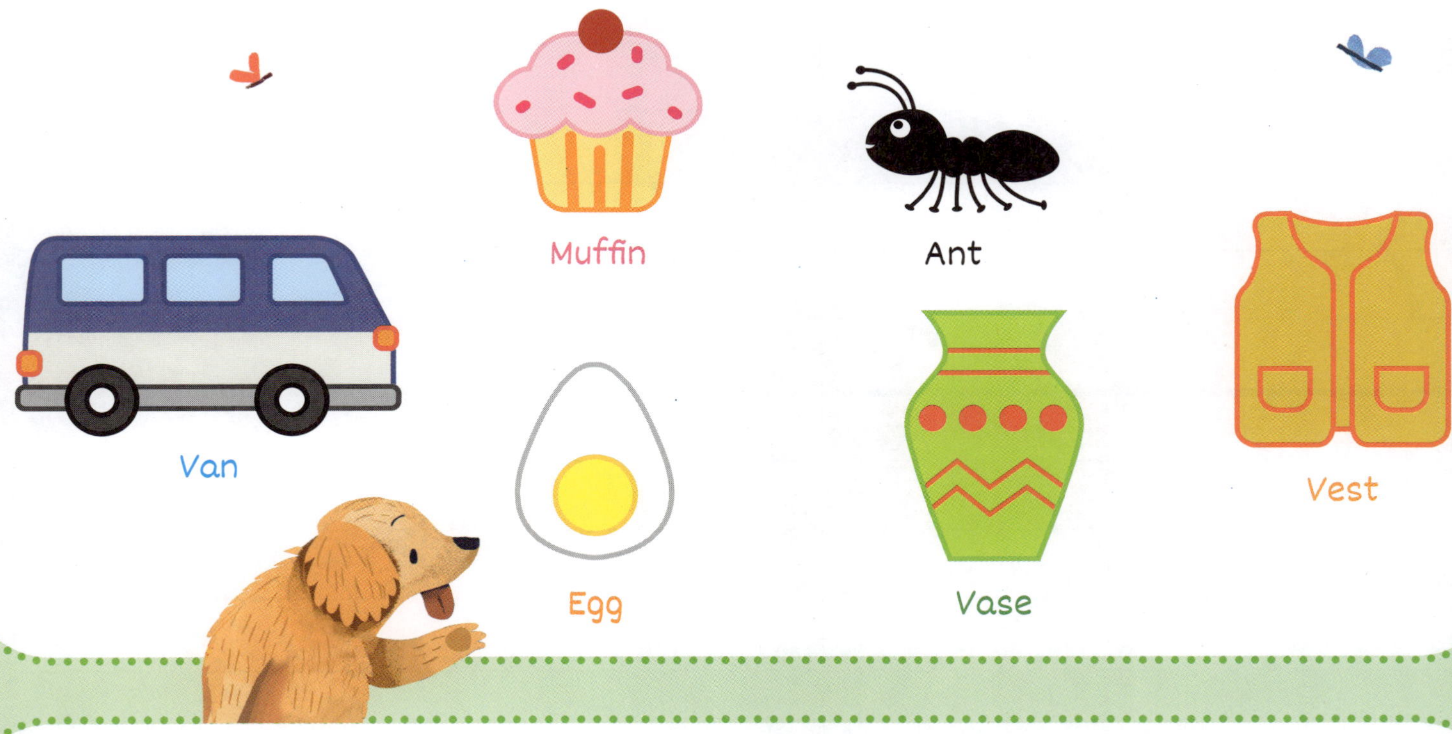

Trace the missing letters to complete the sentence. Then read it out loud.

Violins have four strings.

Use a pencil to trace the letter W.
Then try and write it on your own.

Ww

W w W w

W W W W W

w w w w w w w

Colour the objects that begin with the letter W.

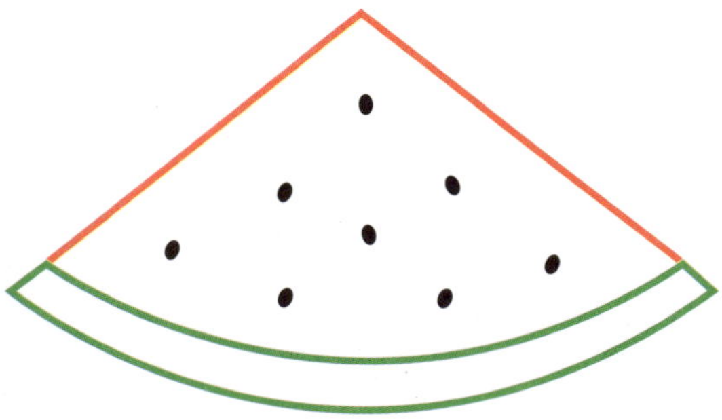

Watermelon

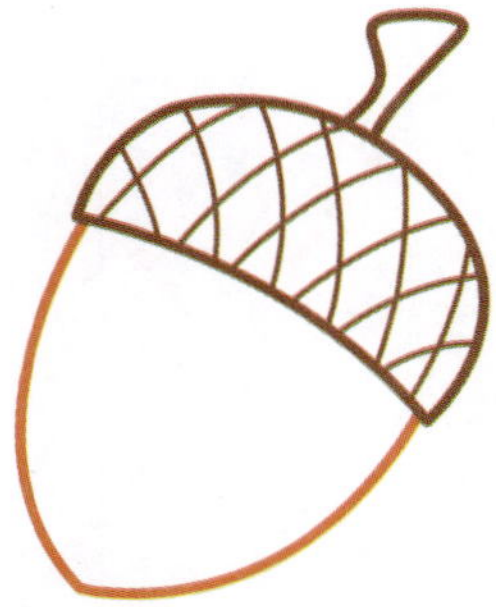

Nut

Ice Cream

Watering Can

Join the circles with capital W and small w to make a pattern.

Q	W	w	s	W	w
w	X	W	w	f	h

Trace the missing letters to complete the sentence. Then read it out loud.

Whales are very large animals.

Use a pencil to trace the letter X.
Then try and write it on your own.

Trace the outline of the stars with capital X and small x.

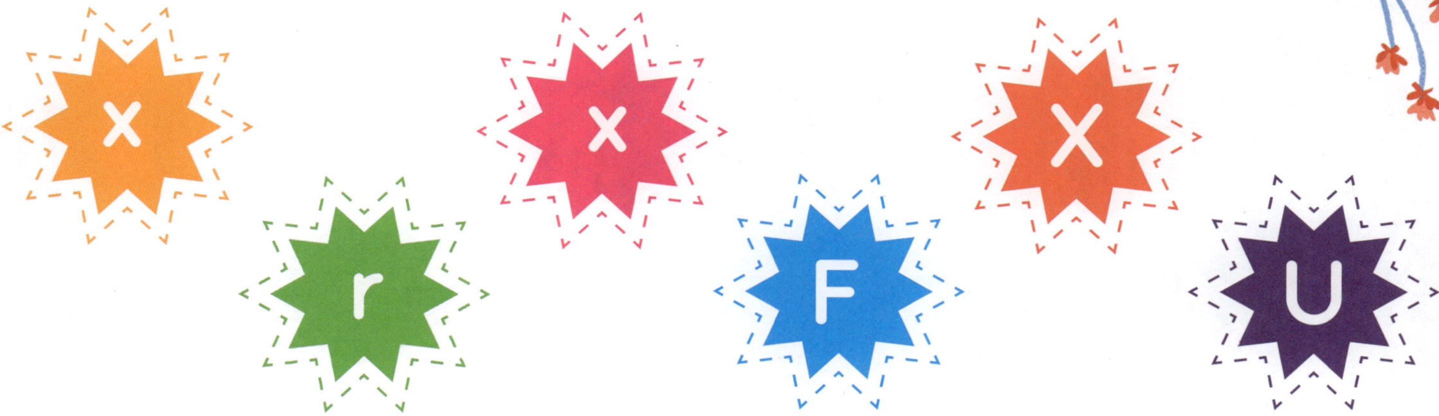

Write capital X or small x to complete the word. Match the word with the correct picture.

___ ylophone   si ___   a ___ e

Trace the missing letters to complete the sentence. Then read it out loud.

Xylophone is a musical instrument.

Use a pencil to trace the letter Y.
Then try and write it on your own.

Yy

Yy Yy

Y Y Y Y Y Y Y

y y y y y y y

Colour the shapes with capital Y and small y.

q R y H Y

Y a Y m y

Identify the object and fill in the box
with capital Y and small y.

☐ o-yo

Pupp ☐

Trace the missing letters to complete the
sentence. Then read it out loud.

Yo-yos are fun to play with.

Use a pencil to trace the letter Z.
Then try and write it on your own.

Zz

Z z Z z

Z Z Z Z Z Z Z

z z z z z z z

Colour the balls with capital Z blue and small z green. One is done for you.

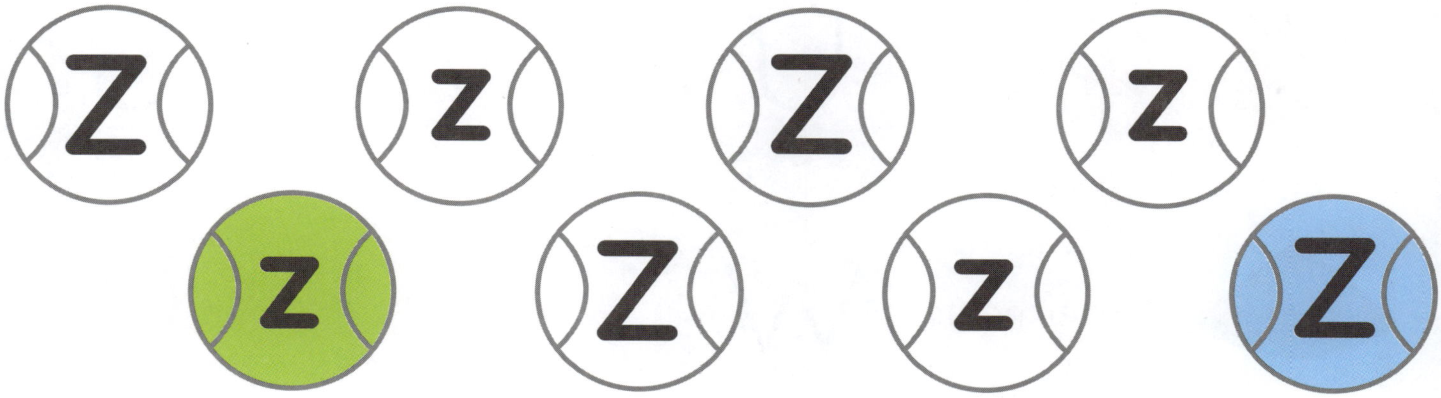

Circle the pictures which begin with the letter Z.

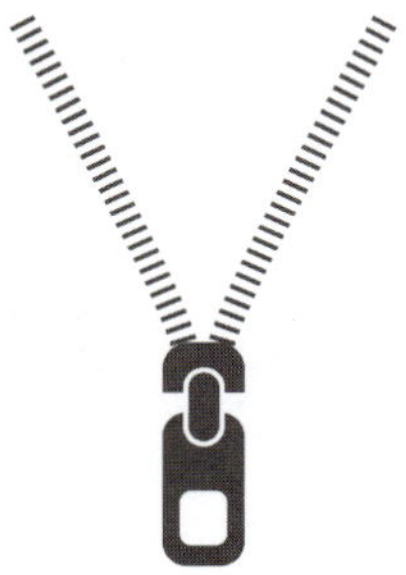

Zip

Jellyfish

Zig Zag

Hammer

Butterfly

Zero

Trace the missing letters to complete the sentence. Then read it out loud.

Zebras are wild animals.

Identify and circle the correct first letter for each of the images below.

	Vest	U	V	S
	Watermelon	W	T	C
	Xylophone	R	G	X
	Zig Zag	J	Z	U

Trace the missing letters to complete the words. Then read them out loud.

very vulture we

won xray yarn

yes zoo zero

Help Gopi reach his friends by marking a path from A to Z.

		A	C	W	K	Q	D	R	U
C	P	B	M	K	U	L	V	P	C
E	T	C	D	E	F	G	H	I	T
J	H	R	O	Y	K	L	Q	J	Y
M	O	B	F	L	A	P	A	K	S
G	T	M	G	I	D	Z	S	L	V
R	D	S	R	Q	P	O	N	M	S
V	F	T	B	F	H	Y	U	F	I
W	H	U	V	W	D	Q	N		
K	S	I	H	X	Y	Z			

Use a pencil to trace the number 1.
Then try and write it on your own.

1

1 1 1

1 1 1 1 1 1 1

Trace the number 1 in words.
Then try and write it on your own.

one one one one

Use a pencil to trace the number 2.
Then try and write it on your own.

2

2 2 2

2 2 2 2 2 2 2

Trace the number 2 in words.
Then try and write it on your own.

two two two two

Use a pencil to trace the number 3.
Then try and write it on your own.

3

3 3 3

3 3 3 3 3 3 3

Trace the number 3 in words.
Then try and write it on your own.

three three three

Use a pencil to trace the number 4.
Then try and write it on your own.

4

4 4 4

4 4 4 4 4 4

Trace the number 4 in words.
Then try and write it on your own.

four four four four

Use a pencil to trace the number 5.
Then try and write it on your own.

5

5 5 5

5 5 5 5 5 5 5

Trace the number 5 in words.
Then try and write it on your own.

five five five five

Use a pencil to trace the number 6.
Then try and write it on your own.

6

6 6 6

6 6 6 6 6 6 6

Trace the number 6 in words.
Then try and write it on your own.

six six six six

Count the objects and write the answer in the box alongside.

Count the different shapes and write the answers in the boxes below.

Write the missing numbers to complete the train.

Use a pencil to trace the number 7.
Then try and write it on your own.

7

7 7 7

7 7 7 7 7 7 7

Trace the number 7 in words.
Then try and write it on your own.

seven seven

Use a pencil to trace the number 8.
Then try and write it on your own.

8

8 8 8

8 8 8 8 8 8 8

Trace the number 8 in words.
Then try and write it on your own.

eight eight eight

Use a pencil to trace the number 9.
Then try and write it on your own.

9

9 9 9

9 9 9 9 9 9 9

Trace the number 9 in words.
Then try and write it on your own.

nine nine nine

Use a pencil to trace the number 10.
Then try and write it on your own.

10

10 10

10 10 10 10 10

Trace the number 10 in words.
Then try and write it on your own.

ten ten ten ten

Look at the scene. Count the animals and objects listed below and write the number in the boxes.

Red Flowers	Rocks	Ducks	Snails	Kites

Blue Flowers

Clouds

Blue Birds

Dog

Butterflies

Use a pencil to trace the number 11.
Then try and write it on your own.

11

11 11

11 11 11 11 11

Trace the number 11 in words.
Then try and write it on your own.

eleven eleven

Use a pencil to trace the number 12.
Then try and write it on your own.

12

12 12

12 12 12 12 12

Trace the number 12 in words.
Then try and write it on your own.

twelve twelve

Use a pencil to trace the number 13.
Then try and write it on your own.

13

13 13

13 13 13 13 13

Trace the number 13 in words.
Then try and write it on your own.

thirteen thirteen

Use a pencil to trace the number 14.
Then try and write it on your own.

14

14 14

14 14 14 14 14

Trace the number 14 in words.
Then try and write it on your own.

fourteen fourteen

Use a pencil to trace the number 15.
Then try and write it on your own.

15

15 15

15 15 15 15 15

Trace the number 15 in words.
Then try and write it on your own.

fifteen fifteen

Use a pencil to trace the number 16.
Then try and write it on your own.

16

16 16

16 16 16 16 16

Trace the number 16 in words.
Then try and write it on your own.

sixteen sixteen

Using a colour pencil, colour the correct number of dots.

13

9

6

12

16

3

Fill in the missing numbers to complete the number line.

1	2		4		6

8		10	11	12	

3				7	8

	8	9	10		

Use a pencil to trace the number 17.
Then try and write it on your own.

17

17 17

17 17 17 17 17

Trace the number 17 in words.
Then try and write it on your own.

seventeen seventeen

Use a pencil to trace the number 18.
Then try and write it on your own.

18

18 18

18 18 18 18 18

Trace the number 18 in words.
Then try and write it on your own.

eighteen eighteen

19

Use a pencil to trace the number 19.
Then try and write it on your own.

19 19

19 19 19 19 19

Trace the number 19 in words.
Then try and write it on your own.

nineteen nineteen

Use a pencil to trace the number 20.
Then try and write it on your own.

20

20 20

20 20 20 20

Trace the number 20 in words.
Then try and write it on your own.

twenty twenty

Write the number that comes after.
One has been done for you.

4	5	14	
10		8	
6		16	

Write the number that comes before.
One has been done for you.

1	2		12
	20		6
	4		15

Write the missing numbers.

1			
	6		
		11	
	14		
			20

Answer key

Page 5

Help Gopi reach the water bowl by colouring the boxes with capital letter A and small letter a.

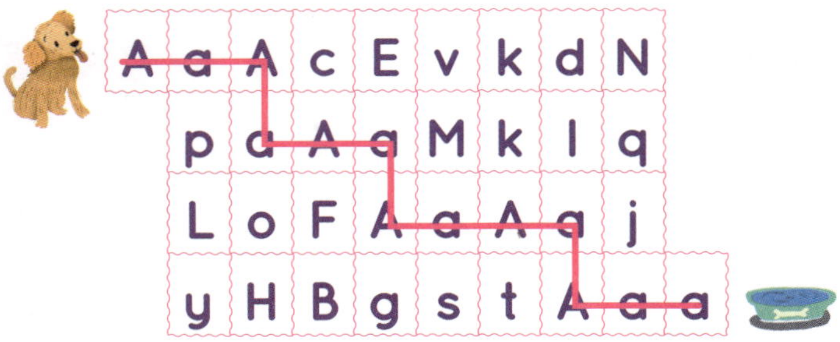

Page 7

Circle the pictures that begin with the letter B.

Page 9

Join the circles with capital C and small c to make a pattern.

Page 13

Write the letters in the correct order in the blank puzzle pieces. Then colour the jigsaw to complete it.

Page 25

Colour the boxes with capital I and small i.

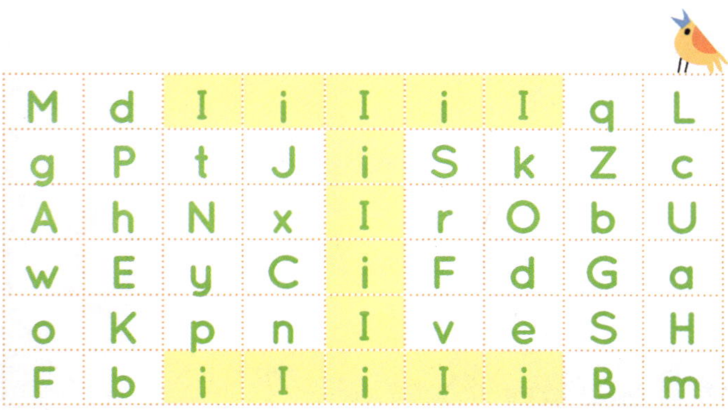

Page 35

Help the squirrel reach the nut by finding the letter M and tracing a path.

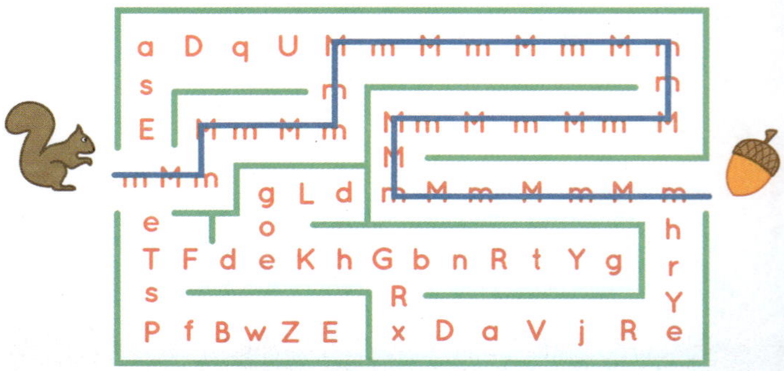

Answer key

Page 53

Help the rabbit reach the carrot by colouring the boxes with capital letter U and small letter u.

	h	V	U	u	U	r	G	k	
	B	p	u	d	u	y	u	U	u
	U	u	U	w	U	t	U	a	
U	u	Z	x	S	u	U	u	M	

Page 67

Help Gopi reach his friends by marking a path from A to Z.

		A	C	W	K	Q	D	R	U
C	P	B	M	K	U	L	V	P	C
E	T	C	D	E	F	G	H	I	T
J	H	R	O	Y	K	L	Q	J	Y
M	O	B	F	L	A	P	A	K	S
G	T	M	G	I	D	Z	S	L	V
R	D	S	R	Q	P	O	N	M	S
V	F	T	B	F	H	Y	U	F	I
W	H	U	V	W	D	Q	N		
K	S	I	H	X	Y	Z			

Page 74

Count the objects and write the answer in the box alongside.

5

4

1

6

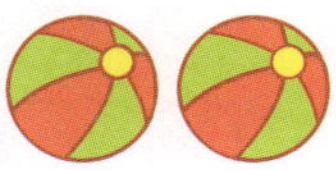

2

3

Page 75

Count the objects and write the answer in the box alongside.

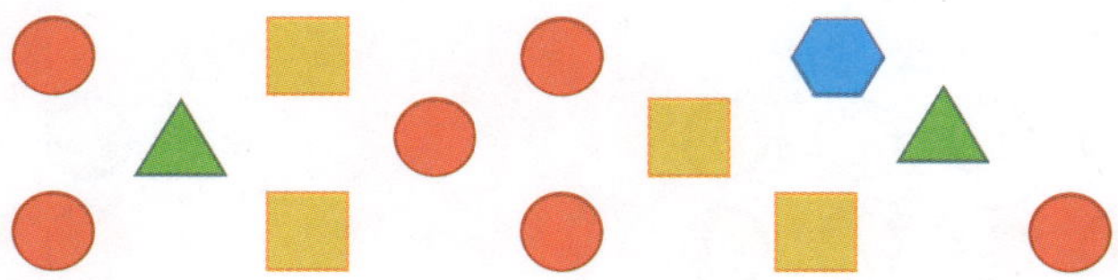

1 2 4 6

Answer key

Page 80-81

Look at the scene. Count the animals and objects listed below and write the number in the boxes.

4	6	8	3	2	9	10	5	1	7
Red Flowers	Rocks	Ducks	Snails	Kites	Blue Flowers	Clouds	Blue Birds	Dog	Butterflies

Page 88

Using a colour pencil, colour the correct number of dots.

Answer key

12

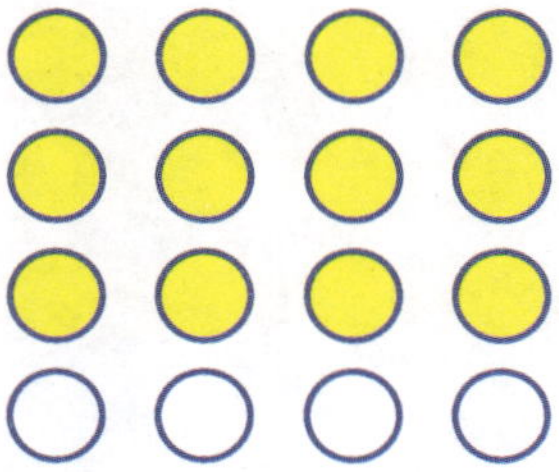

16

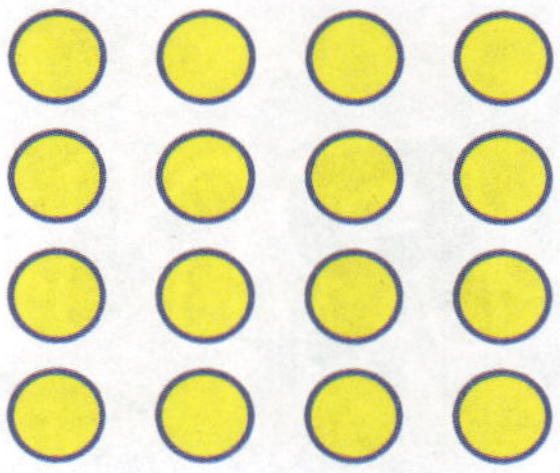

3

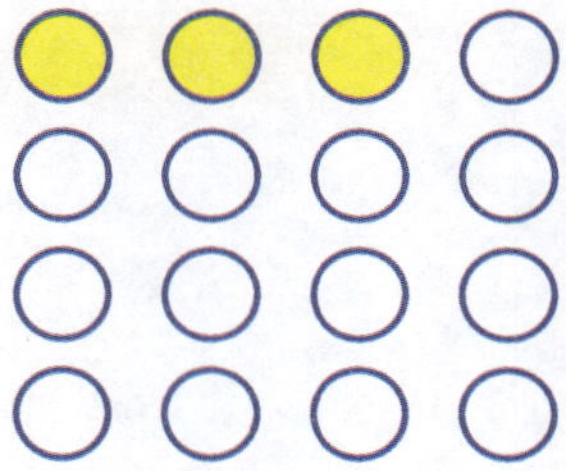

Page 94

Write the number that comes after. One has been done for you.

4	5	14	15
10	11	8	9
6	7	16	17

Write the number that comes before. One has been done for you.

1	2	11	12
19	20	5	6
3	4	14	15

Page 94

Write the number that comes after. One has been done for you.

1 2 3 4 5 6

8 9 10 11 12 13

3 4 5 6 7 8

7 8 9 10 11 12

More in the Gopi Early Learning Range

GOPI'S First Box Of LEARNING

LEARN BASIC CONCEPTS WITH GOPI THROUGH THE TEN BOARD BOOKS IN THIS FIRST BOX OF LEARNING!

FORMAT: Box with ten board books; 24 pages each; 5" x 5"
AGE: 1-5 years
PRICE: ₹ 899

The box and board books have been designed and illustrated by Shamika Chaves. Shamika is a children's book illustrator and graphic designer based in Mumbai. Visit @shamikasdoodles on Instagram or www. shamikasdoodles.com to learn more about her work.

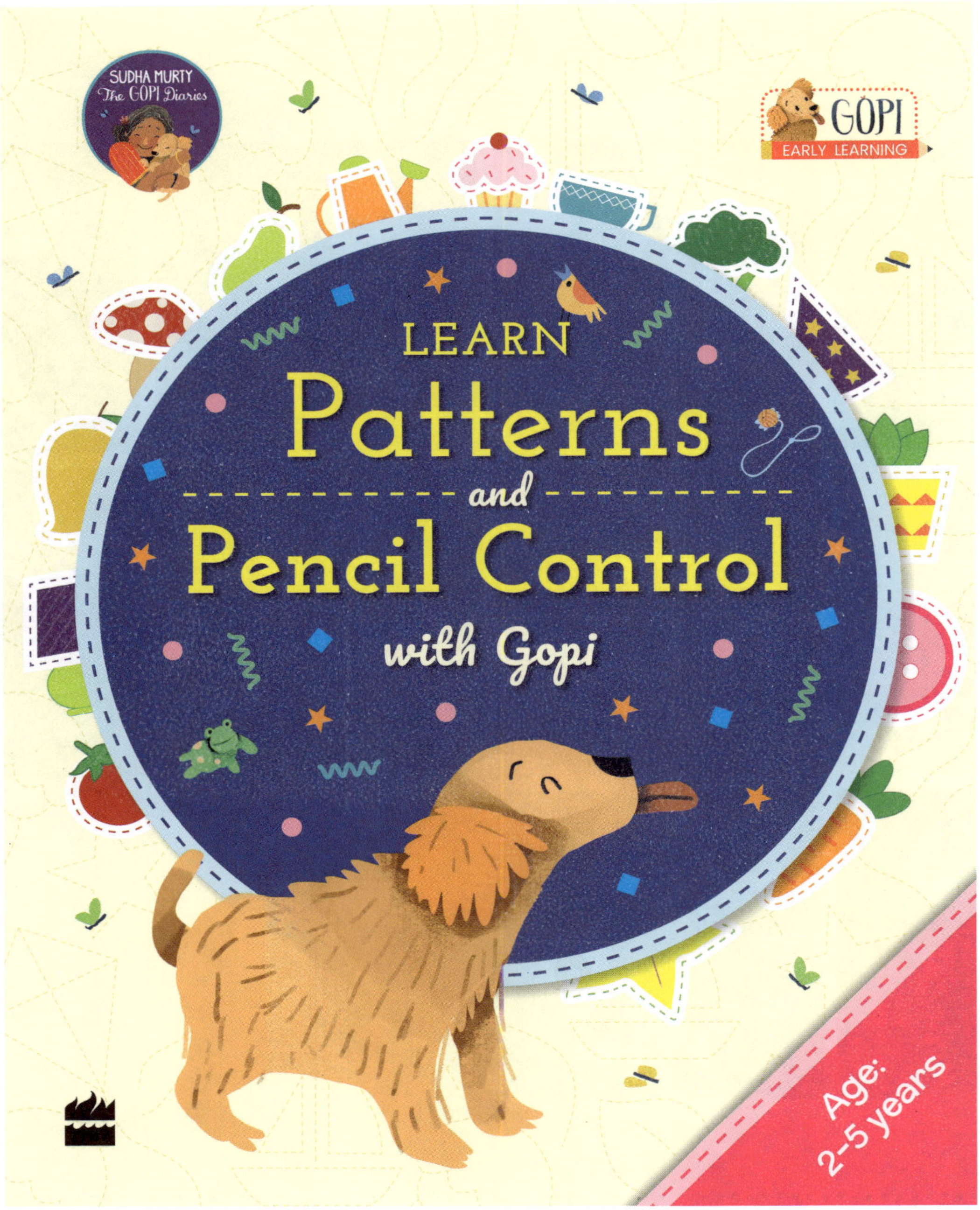

Introduce preschoolers to **writing with the** PATTERNS **and** PENCIL CONTROL exercises in this fun-filled activity book.

This book includes:

- Straight, curvy, zig-zag lines
- Multiple patterns
- Colouring pages
- Puzzles and other activities

Trace these shapes
and then colour them.
Trace the spiral lines.
14
15

Help Gopi catch the kites by
tracing and colouring them.
Trace the leaves and then colour them.
24
25

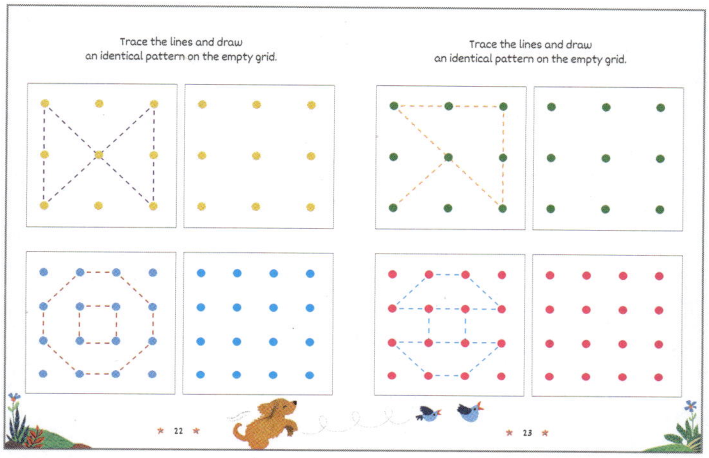
Trace the lines and draw
an identical pattern on the empty grid.
Trace the lines and draw
an identical pattern on the empty grid.
22
23

Help Gopi drive the car by tracing it.
Trace and colour the clouds.
Trace the house
Gopi is visiting.
36
37

Trace these patterns.
Trace these patterns.
26
27

Trace the cake and then colour it.
Trace the candies and then colour them.
52
53

'Gopi has learnt a lot from me, and taught me so much since I became his Ajji. So I am absolutely delighted that young children like you will start your learning journey with Gopi as your naughty and wonderful companion.'

- SUDHA MURTY,
author of the bestselling The Gopi Diaries series

Gopi Early Learning Range

The Gopi Early Learning range has been designed around Gopi, the popular dog from Sudha Murty's bestselling The Gopi Diaries series. From easy recognition to familiar bonding and attachment, character-based books draw children into exploring concepts, activities and learning in companionship with a character they love.

The Gopi Diaries

The Gopi Diaries is a bestselling series for children by Sudha Murty.

In *Coming Home*, the first book in The Gopi Diaries series, Gopi is adopted by his loving, human family. Gopi quickly goes from being a small bundle of white fur to a young pup who understands his world and the people around him faster than they can say 'Gopi!'

In the second book in The Gopi Diaries series, Gopi is stronger, larger, more confident than the little pup he was in the first book, but he is also cheekier and more mischievous! And then comes the day when he faces the biggest surprise of them all ...

The Gopi Diaries series has been illustrated by Sandhya Prabhat.

The third book in The Gopi Diaries series is yet to be published.